You Can Manage People

People

A Step-by-Step Guide on How to Successfully Manage a Variety of People in the Workplace

Table Of Contents

Preface

I woke up one morning feeling all tensed up. I was going to my office where I'd worked for several years, but that morning was different. I wasn't going to work as the lowly carpenter I was known to be, or as a tradesman; that morning I was starting in a new position as Construction Manager! It was quite a huge jump for me and I have always thought of it as an "accident" so to speak.

This book is written to share the practical day-to-day experiences I have had as a successful manager, handling humans, materials, and financial resources in one of the largest construction companies in the UK. The construction company I manage handles projects that are worth millions of pounds and these projects are delivered effectively and efficiently. My daily tasks include managing a large number of workers both men and women, tradesmen, as well as contractors. In my career as a Manager I have been awarded Major National UK House building awards, attending award ceremonies in The House of Commons in London and achieving excellence far beyond what I imagined when I first started as a

Manager. All this and much more, I have achieved without any formal training in management!

In this book, I confidently say "You Can Manage People" to anyone who is willing to make a commitment and diligently follow the same principles I apply daily to my work as a manager. I did not learn these principles in a formal setting, so you can be sure that what you will get in this book is a down-to-earth, no-nonsense, hands-on, practical approach that you can begin to apply to your work and see immediate results. I do not know the theories of management that are currently taught in universities. What I have is know-how which I gained from experience, and that is what is contained here in this book.

The experience shared in this book has helped me manage both the well-educated professionals such as engineers, health and safety advisors and building inspectors; as well as the not-too-formally educated laborer. I have had the experience – challenges and successes – of managing people from a refined background as well as people from a not-so-refined background including ex-convicts. The ability to coordinate people from all walks of life and effectively allocate limited resources to meet your company's goal is what you stand to learn in this practical management guidebook.

Take it from someone who came from a humble beginning and accidentally rose from being a Carpenter to a successful Construction Manager with many years of managerial experience safely tucked under my belt; you can become a successful manager, too regardless of your current level of exposure or experience. Read, study, and apply the steps in this guide to attain your desired level of managerial skill. These steps have been tried and tested repeatedly in the workplace – they work, plain and simple.

Who This Book Is For

In simple terms, this book is for you. It is for managers at all levels; it doesn't matter if you are aspiring to be a manager or if you are an already established one. If it is your responsibility to direct and control one or more staff including the work done in any organization or unit in the organization, there is something in this guidebook for you.

For New Managers

For new managers, it is important for you to realize

that the skill set that got you the job of a manager is different from the skill set needed to succeed as a manager. This book contains the tips your new position as a manager requires for success. Because new managers are often not given adequate coaching or training supports, they tend to blunder and misfire ever so frequently. And sometimes these mistakes may be too costly for both the department they manage and the managers themselves as the mistakes may affect their self-confidence. This book was written with the view to show new managers the likely potholes they need to sidestep to deliver on their mandate.

For Established Managers

If you are already an established manager, this book will serve as the refresher course you rightly need to keep abreast with the practical skills required for handling the daily challenges of your herculean tasks as a manager. From your experience, you do know that the job of taking responsibility for another person's work is no easy task. You know what it feels like to take the fall when things go wrong and to give credit to the team when things turn out great. These are not mere skills anyone can pick up by the roadside. It requires continuous grooming to develop these skills. So, some solid practical tips from a veteran manager who has "been there, done that" wouldn't be a bad idea now, would it?

For Accidental Managers

And if you fall into the category of people I like to term "Accidental Managers" (which I happen to be one, by the way), you will find a database of excellent insights in this book that are capable of propelling you to the next level in your career as a manager. The fear that comes with taking on responsibilities for a position you feel you are not prepared for is a natural one. However, with proper guidance and adequate support, that fear will quickly be turned into the fuel you need to drive you to achieve your goals as a manager. This book has tremendous resources you can draw from to assist you in this accidental position you find yourself. If I can do it and help others to successfully accomplish the same thing, then you too can manage people! Follow the steps, apply them, and watch your accidental career soar high.

For Aspiring Managers (And Those Studying Management)

From all the careers you could possibly choose, you decided to opt for being a manager and you have taken the bold step to study management. Congratulations! Note, however, your aspirations and studies may get you a job with a title as manager, but it takes more than that to qualify you as a successful manager. The daily grind that comes with your chosen career requires you to have a heads-up even before you complete your studies. Therefore, this book will be one of your greatest assets and companion as it contains the best practical pieces of advice on management. Unlike most books and study materials that you will discard after your studies, this one will stay with you even if you choose to change careers. After all, you still need to manage your personal affairs even if you do not manage people and resources in a company.

For those who wish to broaden their horizon regarding management, and for those who choose to acquire managerial skills in addition to their present skill sets, this book will not be just an eye opener, but also the go-to, practical coach you truly need.

I can boldly make the statement that this book is worth every penny you have invested in it and even more.

How to Use This Book

This book has been deliberately written in such a way that it breaks down the lessons into actionable steps; it is designed as a step-by-step guidebook which can be used as a practical manual. It is highly recommended that you take the time to read the book from start to finish in chronological order at least once to grasp a clear understanding of the entire context. However, you can choose to jump to a specific chapter that deals with a topic you wish to understand better.

For ease-of-use, each chapter contains a summary of its major points. This comes at the chapter's end as bullet points. You can easily refer to the bullet points if you are short on time and urgently need to consult this material. Let me add, however, that if you have not studied a specific topic or chapter in its entirety, the bullet points may not give you the details you need since they simply serve as short summaries of points already discussed in the chapter.

As you prepare yourself to be a successful manager,

this book will serve as an indispensable tool both for you and your organization. And yes, it takes adequate preparation to become successful. You should remember that one way or the other, you are preparing; you either prepare to succeed or you fail to prepare which is the same as preparing to fail. The former (preparing to succeed) is the focus of this book.

Introduction

The task of managing one's own personal life is challenging; add to that the extra work of managing other people and directing their efforts towards a common goal, and you will agree it is not an easy task to manage humans. A lot of people spend several years studying how to manage people, yet when they get to the actual workplace where what they have studied needs to be applied, they find to their dismay that the real-life workplace is completely different from what was presented in the pages of their books.

Humans are unique as well as dynamic – that is why outmoded theories of management may not work well in our rapidly changing world. Managers are discovering first-hand that the workplace dynamics require them to do further work than they have been led to believe.

In this book, I am taking the unconventional path to present well-tested ideas that will cut off unnecessary gibberish usually offered in the name of management tips.

Since we are looking at how to successfully manage people in the workplace, we are not going to concern ourselves with too many definitions and theorizing; I have intentionally left out those aspects to the formal institutions since they are good at theories. This material is very pragmatic – it is the daily steps required to effectively manage people in a real-live workplace, not a classroom managerial lecture.

Your report as a manager is glaringly evident. The very people you manage are your report. What is the performance level of the majority of your subordinates? What does that performance level say about you as their manager? How do they relate to you? What feedback do you get from them? Are you their boss? Are you their leader? These and many more questions hold the answers and are pertinent to uncovering the keys to your success as a manager.

What you will get in this book is authentic, doable, and simple. I said simple, but you should know that "simple" does not necessarily translate to easy. I do not promise you that after reading this book, your managerial skills will automatically transform overnight. However, I do know this for sure; those who will commit to the steps and ideas shared in this book will see tremendous changes in the people they manage and in the results their unit, department, or organization achieves.

If the information in this book holds true for only me, then it would be considered a fluke. But a considerable number of others have also applied this same wealth of information I am sharing with you, and it has worked and is still working for them. I did not learn these methods in a conventional way. As a matter of fact, I did not become a manager by rising through the ranks. I was a carpenter who suddenly "fell into" the role of a manager. It was a blessing and a nightmare – a blessing because it elevated me from a simple tradesman; a nightmare because I was not formally prepared for it. By following the exact tips and steps I have written in this book, I became a truly successful Construction Manager. And if I can do it, you can manage people, too.

Managing people will no longer be a dreaded task for you after studying and applying what you learn from this book – that is my guarantee! Several people who have discovered the seeming magical steps this book has to offer have scaled up their production, reinvented their businesses, drastically reoriented their organization's route to a more positive outlook, and have had huge successes with resolving their staff issues more amicably.

You may not be able to satisfy every single worker you manage – as a matter of fact, no one can. However, when you apply the contents of this book, you will be certain of balancing the commitment you have to your organization and your duty to the people you manage.

The time for you to improve your managerial skills is right now. It is time to put behind your mundane theories that have no bearing within the modern workplace. It is time to take a dive into the pool of uncommon tips that this book offers.

Chapter 1:

Build Your Power Team

The pages of a new book on my shelf were coming off. There was an error in the spine during the book production. Although the book was relatively new (and expensive for its size and contents, I must add), it was poorly produced. Something about that book sitting on my shelf somehow reminds me of one key ingredient to effectively manage people; no matter the size, cost, and purpose of an organization, if the spine of the organization is faulty, you have no organization. The spine of a book holds the book together; just as the spine or foundation of an organization holds it together.

So, what is this figurative spine I speak of? Your power team is your organization's spine or foundation. And even if your leadership role does not extend to cover the entire organization, your little team you head in your unit or department is your spine; and the stronger the spine, the stronger your unit, department or organization.

Question: How can a newly appointed manager who is probably new in an organization or department build a power team? How will an accidental manager know who to place on his team?

Essentially, these questions are saying: how does one build a power team? In this chapter, we shall explore the various doable steps to take to build a powerful team that will be a formidable spine for your unit, department, or organization at large.

First Things First: Drop the Title

You were newly promoted or appointed as the manager. Congratulations! Now drop the title, roll up your sleeves and get down to work. Your first task is to identify the heads of each subunit under your managerial purview and bring them together with the aim of building them up – actually molding them into your generals so to speak. However, the approach involved in building or molding them into your generals will not include a military approach, rather, the reverse is the case.

The sooner you realize that there is a huge difference between your personal power and the power that comes with your title, the earlier you will make progress in creating a formidable team. It is your ability to separate your personal power from the power your position wields that distinguishes you as a true leader. Always remember that true leaders do not need promotions or titles to function. Their role is more important to them than their titles.

One who manages people is a focal point. Even if you were unnoticeable or a friend to all in your department, the very moment you assume the position of a manager, to lead others, you automatically become the center of attention. All eyes are suddenly on you. They want to see the real you; they want to know how power will affect your personality. It will serve you well to use those early periods of your new position to focus on doing what will help you succeed, rather than basking in the euphoria of the new position. Before your title gets into your head and makes you feel like you're now the boss of them, drop it. There will be more than enough time for that later. A huge responsibility has been placed on your shoulders. Realize that you cannot do it alone and begin immediately seeking capable hands to assist you in your new arduous task.

How you choose your team members depends on the kind of manager you are; a new manager or an established manager. To avoid costly mistakes in your career, take the time to study and apply these tips according to your level.

For Rookies

If you are completely new to the organization and are saddled with the responsibility of a manager, or it is your first time handling the job of managing people, I strongly suggest you sit and talk with the subunit or departmental heads. They will be the initial members of your team. With time, you will be able to properly appraise them and designate or drop members of the team as needed. Ensure that in your first sit-down with them, you clearly and unambiguously communicate your goals and your expectations. But do not do so in a boss-subordinate manner. Let your style convey to them that each person has a share in the responsibility of growing the organization, and each person's role is as vital as the next person's. Let your style pass a clear message to them that you see them all as equals. Remember, there is no second chance to make a first impression so put your best foot forward in this first meeting.

One more thing, do not talk *to* your team, rather, have a talk *with* them. Impress upon them that you are completely open to prompt feedbacks. Give ample room for them to express their opinions and communicate back to you what they also expect from you. This part of team building is very crucial. Be sure to take their communication seriously. It is of utmost importance for you to pay attention and listen to what your team has to say. If you must succeed in your new position as a manager of people, you must train yourself in the art of paying attention to your people (more on this in chapter four).

For Old Dogs

For established managers who are looking to build their own organization, here's a quick tip: take all the time you need to handpick quality people that will make up your team. The temptation to get your company up and running in the shortest possible time can be very strong and push you to hire unqualified persons just to get your organization packed full of human bodies. Unless you aim to boast of having the largest staff on your workforce, the rush to bring people on board is better avoided. When building your team, it is best to slowly hire people, conduct well it interviews and take the necessary time to ough background check on each person coming on as a member of your team. Always remember that the spine of your book matters a lot if you do not want the pages to come off easily.

Create Leaders

For your team to qualify as a power team, they should be made up of leaders. You do not expect to be called a true leader if the best you can do is make followers out of people. Give your people the opportunity to become leaders themselves, that's how to know a good leader. In my experience, I have found the following as ways to build a power team of great leaders:

Here's the Game Plan, any Better Ideas?

Present what you want to be done to your team – communicate to them your game plan; your goals, then ask for their ideas. A manager who often points out problems without drawing up a general idea what a solution should look like, comes across as clueless and incompetent. It is not enough to say, "We have a problem"; what thoughts have you given to problem before bringing it to the table? Your thoughts about the problem will certainly reflect in the game plan you present before your power team. It is better to present a game plan, even if not well thought-out than to present nothing. The reason you have a power team, to begin with, is to help you do the work of thinking from different points of view.

When you present your ideas as plans that can be improved upon, or rather as plans that *should* be improved upon, your team knows you are including them in the decision-making process of the organization. They will begin to think outside the box – the box of their job description – and proffer brilliant ideas beyond what is expected of them. I cannot overemphasize the need for including this idea in your manager kit. It will result in bringing out the best from your team.

When I took up the role of a manager, I knew there were lots of things about managing people that I did not know, but one thing I did learn fast was this idea of placing my game plan before my team and asking for their opinions. Sometimes, it was difficult to accept what they put forward because that would mean entirely throwing out my ideas. But I quickly learned that no one individual's idea is better than a power team's idea. My mentor always told me, "If you have all the brilliant ideas, what's the point in building a power team?" I figured he was right. I did create a power team because I wanted refined ideas that could move the organization forward. I did not put up a team of mere "rubber stamps" who would just nod and agree to everything I brought up. And this brings me to my next tip.

No Yes-Men; No Cankerworms Either

Look out for those individuals on the team who have nothing to offer aside from "yessing" all your ideas; they are extra luggage. The earlier you replace them, the better for your organization. You'll know them by their vigorous nods agreeing to every word that comes out of your mouth. You'll know them by the look in their eyes when there is a decision to be taken and they hesitate, so that they can be sure of what side you tend to lean before they make their decision. You will know them by the unsolicited support they appear to eagerly show you. And you will know them in the way they tend to hang around you like a puppy waiting for its master.

When I say to get rid of those on your team "who have

nothing to offer," I am not suggesting that your team members must all continuously contribute barrages of brilliant ideas only. Give room for constructive criticisms too and never look at the one who counters a seemingly bright idea as a wet blanket. Learn to take counter suggestions or opinions as a sign that your team is looking at the issue at hand from all possible angles. However, be wary of the pessimists; they may be disguised as people offering constructive criticisms. A sure way to detect them is that they never seem to have a positive opinion about any issue. Their views always tear down the issue at-hand without offering constructive alternative ideas. Such people have the capacity to bring down your entire team. If you intend to keep your power team sane and in one piece, do away with such cankerworms as soon as you identify them. It is better to have a few good heads on your team that can propel your organization forward than to cram the team full of individuals who take pleasure in tearing apart.

Keep the Circle as Small as Possible

Moreover, it is not how large your power team is that matters. I have come to discover first-hand that the fewer members on my power team, the better results I get. When you have too many people on your team, you tend to duplicate functions or make one member's role grossly overlap into the function of another member.

It is true that to succeed as a manager you should consider the ideology that two good heads are always better than one; hence you need others to succeed. However, when building your power team, you should balance that ideology with the perspective that two is company and three is a crowd, so you don't go stuffing your team with everyone who has an appearance of a "good head."

To help you pick relevant people into your power team, always think in terms of your strength and weaknesses. If you identify someone who has one of your positive qualities – your strength – leave the person out of your team. You already have what he or she has. There's no point duplicating that quality. Be on the lookout for people who can do what you cannot do – people who complement your weaknesses and select the best out of them. This way, you keep your team as small as possible with each person playing uniquely relevant roles that have a greater impact on the entire organization.

Set the Ball Rolling... and Get Out of th

Once you clearly communicate your intention ᴜ ᴊ team, you will do well to get out of their way and let them function. You cannot expect someone to perform at their best when you are constantly breathing down their necks. By allowing your handpicked team to function without constant interference or choking supervision, you are conveying a message that loudly says, "I trust your capability to do your part well." This is one of the greatest motivations you can give to your power team.

Again, the way you communicate your intention to your team matters a lot. To illustrate this point, let us examine this example of two seemingly same statements conveying two very different messages: "I want you to get this done right now," and, "Let us see how we can get this done as soon as possible."

The former loudly screams to your team that you are the boss, and they must do exactly as you say – no more, no less. It shuts down their willingness to go the extra mile. It cuts out any idea that they may go beyond the job description. That statement puts you in their way of thinking. Even if they want to give their best, you are there standing in their way telling them not to go beyond what you have asked of them – "get *this* done."

On the other hand, the latter statement silently says to them, all hands are on deck on this one; from boss to subordinate. It gives them a sense of belonging. It tells them you have rolled up your sleeves to work with them on this. "Let *us see how we*," is a powerful way of saying your ideas are welcome, I look forward to receiving them.

Once you get out of their way, you are in effect getting out of your own way, too!

Summary of Key Points

The tips you have learned in this chapter include:

1. Your role is not just a title. Your most important first role as a manager is to build your power team.

2. Your success as a manager largely hinges on how strong your spine – your power team – is. Take the time to carefully select those who complement your weaknesses. Let every member of your power team play a unique role; there should be no duplication of

functions.

3. Allow leaders you have created to use their initiatives; their best comes to the forefront that way.

4. Let the few who make up your power team know that you value their ideas and opinions by giving them the chance to contribute positively to your plans. And be open to constructive criticisms.

Chapter 2:

All About You

Effectively managing people begins and ends with you. You cannot be focused on leading other people and forget to develop yourself. You must set aside enough time to improve your attitudes and character traits if you plan to make progress as a manager. A manager is saddled with enormous responsibilities; there is no room for excuses. The good and bad, the successes and failures, all end on your table. Remember, when things go wrong, it is your fault, and when it goes right, it is the team's effort.

Study the following key traits with the aim of absorbing them.

Have a Presence

How do you feel when someone your regard highly walks into a room? How does it feel to be in the presence of someone with a personality that magnetizes? That is what it means to have a positive presence.

Having a positive presence goes beyond acting or putting up a facade. It must come from within. Think about how you want people to feel when they are around you or when you walk into a room. Feel that way about yourself long before you walk into that room. If the feeling is not in you, you cannot give it to others.

You cannot give what you do not have. You cannot give the people you manage assurance when what they read from you is a lack of self-confidence. What you radiate speaks louder than the words you speak, and people can and really do pick up what you radiate. They can sense it no matter how you try to mask it. If your presence does not exude confidence, you probably aren't going to have a team to lead for very long.

I recommend you practice the kind of effect you want to have on people before you are scheduled to meet with them. Have the conversations, the meetings, or the presentations in your mind and see yourself doing great. Feel as if these imagined events are actually occurring and you are truly confident and secure in your performance. How does the tone of your voice sound? What gestures do you see yourself making? Are you holding the attention of your audience? This is what some refer to as visualization. To have a powerful presence – to create a lasting effect or influence on people – it all starts in your head.

Be Highly Organized

It goes without saying that being messy or shambolic in your personal lifestyle will reflect in your work, too. Effective managers are well organized at home and in the workplace. Being highly organized starts with daily practice and before long it becomes a habit. Let's look at some tips on how to be organized.

Prioritizing

Obviously, each day, there are lots of things screaming for your attention. A great way to handle them is to ask yourself which of them is most important. Treat the most important ones first and, either handle the less important ones later, or delegate them to someone else. If you jump into your day and try to fix things in the order they come, this chaotic approach will throw you off-balance and leave you exhausted without having achieved much of anything.

Following a To-Do List

I did not say to have a To-Do List. It's easy to have it. Following it, however, is a different ball game. If you won't be committed to a To-Do List what's the point in having it? As much as possible, follow your To-Do List. In exceptional cases, you may have to deviate a bit from your list especially when there is an urgent, priority task to be handled which you haven't factored into your To-Do List. Remember that your To-Do List is not carved in stone; give room for a little bit of flexibility.

Take a Break

You are not a robot! If you misconstrue being a workaholic with being efficient and highly organized, you may end up sentencing yourself to a lifetime of routines. Take time to give yourself a well-deserved break. Take a walk, go to the movies, get a massage – just do something out of your routine or busy schedule. It's a way of rewarding yourself for being organized.

If You Begin It, Complete It

Half-done assignments show disorganization. Put your heart into every task from start to finish. If you complete just one task per day, you would have the satisfaction of having at least one thing properly done. That is by far better than having lots of tasks started without completing any. Having lots of unfinished tasks makes it difficult for you to concentrate on one particular task that needs finishing.

No Clutter

When you walk into the office of a manager, take a look at his or her table or desk. A table or desk with files and papers littered about is a sign of disorganization. Keep your working space uncluttered by sorting papers.

Reminders

Calendars, Alarms, Notepads, etc are all things that are within the immediate vicinity of an organized person. Since you are human and may forget important stuff, it is a good practice to set reminders and alarms using whatever means are available to you.

Be Positive

There is nothing more depressing than looking up to a boss who has a very negative outlook about everything. People will avoid you like a plague when they notice you are always pessimistic. No matter how bleak a situation appears, a leader is one whom the people look up to for a ray of hope. I am not suggesting that a leader should give false hope. Rather, I am of the strong opinion that a leader looks for a way around, above, or through the situation. A good manager inspires hope by bringing the people's attention to the positive aspects of whatever situation that is before them.

Let your focus be on creating solutions. If you steer people away from looking at the problems to concentrating on ways to solve problems and improve on solutions, they will naturally gravitate towards you. You will be like a magnet attracting them because people tend to identify with those who proffer solutions than those who point out problems.

Someone once said to the people he was leading, "we are doomed!" That statement killed whatever last ray of hope his people had of coming out of that seemingly hopeless situation. A good manager will say something along these lines, "It's just a temporal setback. Somehow, I know that together we will find a way out of this."

Be Motivational

For you to motivate others, you must first motivate yourself. Be the kind of person you will want to emulate. When you can look up to the standard of yourself, then you can truly motivate others. Set standards for yourself and don't settle for less. When your people see how committed you are to your ideas, they will naturally fall-in behind you.

In trying to motivate the people you manage, remember that different things motivate different people. Using one form of motivation for every member of your team is a grave error. You need to take the time to learn and understand what makes each one of your people tick. When you rightly understand this, motivating the people you lead will progress from mere routine motivations to sincere nudges that are capable of propelling them to greater performances.

Delegate

Develop your people in such a way that they do not need you to always be around to function properly. And one way to do that is to assign them some of your duties. This has a dual benefit. First, it builds up your people; it makes them learn how to perform those tasks better since they will be performing them in your stead. They know the tasks must be performed to the standards of a leader to measure up. In so doing, they will most oftentimes exceed your expectations. You have provided an excellent platform for them to bring to fore something that even they may not have known was present in them.

And secondly, delegating relieves you of tasks that someone else can handle, so that you can focus on other tasks. You cannot be everywhere at the same time, so you must delegate to succeed. As you delegate tasks, you are in effect creating leaders.

Be Driven

Many people often confuse "to be driven" with a workaholic. There is a world of difference between being a workaholic and being someone who is driven.

Others mistake the quality of being driven to mean one is self-centered. To be driven is not being self-centered.

A workaholic works long hours because they are addicted to work; they have a strong compulsion to work. It may be a sign that they have internal struggles which they try to hide from by using their work as an excuse. It is worthy of note that working long hours doesn't necessarily translate to achieving a corresponding level of positive results.

A self-centered person focuses mainly on what they stand to gain regardless of who loses in the process. It is difficult for such a person to effectively manage people, let alone lead a team. These are not the qualities of one who is driven.

To be driven means you are alive to what it is you can accomplish. You know only you can put a limit to the things you can accomplish. It is this knowing that propels you to continually raise the bar for yourself. You do not necessarily work hard and long hours; you simply work smart and more efficiently. You do not give up in the face of seemingly insurmountable obstacles. Your sight is set so high that obstacles only serve to be a stepping-stone for you.

A driven person draws inspiration from the achievements of others and uses that as motivation or fuel to press on. A self-centered person only feels jealous or threatened by the achievements of others. And a workaholic is probably going to bury their heads in work just to distract themselves from the realities before them.

A manager who spends long hours at work may think they are extra committed to work, but that could send the wrong message to their team. What they may read from such behavior is that you cannot balance your work life and your personal or family life. And how would you think they will respond if you were to require them to put in extra hours at work? "He thinks we don't care about family because he has no regard for his."

Be a Leader

It is common knowledge that a good manager should come across as a leader and not a boss. However, what is not common is how to be a leader. Does one become a leader when promoted to the post of a manager? If having the title of manager automatically translates to a leader, who then is a boss? And, by the way, is being a boss a bad thing?

Who is a Leader?

In the setting of a workplace, and in the context of this book, a leader oversees others. But then, isn't that who a boss is? Technically, a manager, a leader, and a boss are all one and the same. We are simply using different terms to describe the same thing – someone who leads others or manages others. However, the term "leader" and "boss" have become adjectives that are used to qualify a manager. So, we can accurately say "that a manager is a true leader," or "that a manager is just an overbearing boss." I said all of that to say that your attitude as a manager is what makes others regard you as a leader or a boss.

Are You a Boss or a Leader?

The following tips will give you a brief description of twenty-one differences in the attitudes that make someone a boss or a leader.

1. A boss is like a cold robot – very impersonal; he or she is not friendly and sees the people he or she

manages as subordinates. A leader, on the other hand, is considerate; they understand, they feel, they are humane.

2. A boss tends to intimidate subordinates, thereby, instilling fear. A leader does their best to earn their team's loyalty and respect.

3. A boss admonishes and disciplines. A leader advises and suggests course-corrective actions.

4. A boss takes all the credit and praise. There is no "team success" from a boss. On the flip side, a leader gives credit to the combined effort of the team.

5. A boss insists on getting results, the means notwithstanding. A leader encourages team performance without undue pressure.

6. A boss will often instruct people to "go get it done." A leader involves his or herself in the task at hand by saying, "let's go get it done."

7. A boss draws attention to the flaws and faults of people. A leader focuses on the innate abilities of people. They ensure they highlight your strengths.

8. A boss tends to force, coerce or push people. A

leader does just that – lead; no coercion, just gentle nudges, and encouragements.

9. A boss views issues from the "pixel level". They often consider immediate results or short-term effects. A leader considers issues by looking at the "big picture" and not just the pixels. They consider long-term effects.

10. A boss points accusing fingers. They do not take the fall for failure. A leader accepts responsibility for failures.

11. A boss hardly listens. They have an annoying tendency to dominate conversations. In fact, with a boss, it is not a conversation, but a monologue. A leader, on the other hand, listens, pays attention, and contributes to the conversation.

12. A boss stands aside to oversee how the task is done. A leader gets involved in the task and ensures the team achieves its goal.

13. A boss asserts themselves by attending to minute details in management. They tend to micromanage. A leader often delegates functions while they attend to more challenging issues.

14. A boss has their language filled with this word spelled with a single letter: "I". That is all that matters. A leader's vocabulary always features the word, "We."

15. A boss takes ego-based actions, protecting their exaggerated self-image at all cost. A leader is not afraid to show that they are humans with flaws.

16. A boss considers people as tools or mere resources to be used and dumped. A leader builds up people. Leaders are concerned about the personal development of their team; hence, they seek ways to encourage and nurture their natural abilities.

17. A boss has the answer to all things. A leader asks for suggestions that will best handle issues arising.

18. A boss gives orders. A leader provides guidance and offers assistance. They tend to coach people.

19. A boss values his or herself far and above the team; their focus is usually self-centered. A leader places tremendous value on their team. Their focus is usually on the team.

20. A boss chooses a favorite – a sacred cow. A leader promotes impartiality and equality among all.

21. A boss always says, "I know." They have nothing to learn. A leader is continually learning. They have the willingness and are open to learning.

Understand That You Are Learning and Always Will Be

Earlier in the preceding page, we pointed out that a leader is continually learning. Any manager who stops learning has succeeded in truncating their own growth. It is a grave mistake on the part of any manager to assume that they know it all. No matter how good you are in any individual area or on a specific subject or topic, you cannot know it all because there is such a thing called change. Everyone should know that the only thing constant is change. And since this is true, even the issue you are very proficient in is subject to change; meaning, you should be willing to learn a new way of doing what you once knew so well.

Every now and then, new managers (and in some cases, old ones, too) tend to act in ways that suggest they are not open to learning. Study the tips below and avoid falling into these mistakes.

Common Mistakes

1. It is not uncommon for many new managers to want to show that they know it all. They feel the need to prove themselves as qualified to assume that position, so they are everywhere at the same time throwing their "know it all" mentality around and mostly leaving behind mistakes in their wake.

It is of great importance to recognize that your job as a manager is to build up others, not to show them that you know how to perform their jobs. You *were* good at their job, which was what earned you your promotion, to begin with. Now your task is no longer to display your previous expertise but to help others grow and develop. Your attention should not be on emphasizing how good you are or how knowledgeable you are, rather learn to concentrate on bringing out the skills and abilities of the people you manage so they can become experts, too.

2. Closely related to the above is the unnecessary eagerness many new managers tend to have in changing the status quo all at once. For God's sakes, the status quo brought you to your new position! At least respect that. If everything prior to your

"assumption of office" was wrong, then your promotion or appointment was wrong. It is the attitude of "knowing it all" that usually prompts such actions.

A better way to create a peaceful and lasting change is to seek out suggestions and opinions from your team members on ways to modify areas of their jobs that will result in effectiveness and efficiency. A complete overhaul done to the entire system at once may result in unpalatable changes. A manager should communicate his or her planned changes to their team and be open to welcome suggestions that are better and more encompassing than he or she has thought up. It is the attitude of unwillingness to learn that makes a manager avoid ideas that may challenge his or her opinions.

3. When managers are unwilling to learn, they commonly make the mistake of operating all alone. Aside from not involving their team in decision-making, they also leave out their bosses or senior management which were instrumental to their promotion. Solo actions and independent operations send out a loud and clear message to senior management that you are not willing to receive

guidance or to be coached. There is no point trying to prove that you can function independently; it gets you nowhere fast! You are part of your own team too, and, for the team to function properly, team members are mutually dependent.

Find a Mentor/Coach

I blundered through my first few days of finding myself in the position of a manager; falling and rising and basically repeating the same process over and again. If I were to last in that position and if there were to be a company existing to keep me in that position, I had to quickly find a permanent solution. Fortunately for me, I found my solution in a mentor.

The truth is, no one is a storehouse of all knowledge. And no matter how good and proficient you are in what you do, there are several other aspects you know practically nothing about. I learned that if I wanted to do well and succeed in an area I had little or no idea about, I needed to find someone who was already good in that aspect and simply follow their example.

No matter the number of books you study about management in a formal setting, the art of managing people is a completely different ballgame in real-life than it is on the pages of a book. I strongly suggest you get a mentor or a coach if you intend to succeed as a manager. Remember, you are learning and always will be. A mentor's worth is invaluable, and they can give you insights and suggestions you could never have come up with on your own.

For new managers, finding a coach or a mentor may be easier. Look for someone in senior management whose managerial style you admire and wish to draw inspiration from and emulate them. It isn't such a bad idea if you had a little chat with them over lunch and ask them to be your coach or mentor. Or simply ask what their secret to success is. I have found that most good leaders are open to sharing their tips and tricks usually for free if only you have the courage to ask and are willing to put to practice what they share with you.

It will be an effort in futility to seek out a mentor or coach and not use their tips. You not only end up wasting both their time and your time, but you also waste precious knowledge and information.

Spend quality time with a mentor, coach or a friend who inspires you. With time, they tend to rub off on you.

Summary of Key Points

The tips you have learned in this chapter include:

1. You can be a manager who is seen as a leader or a boss. There's a world of difference between the two. Study them and choose wisely.

2. No one is a repository of all knowledge. Be open and willing to learn. A mentor or a coach will keep you focused on your goals – find one and apply their tips.

3. Do not overwork yourself. You cannot be everywhere at the same time. Effectively managing people requires that you trust them enough to delegate duties.

4. Exude confidence. Let your presence be felt without coming across as domineering.

Chapter 3:

Creating Relationships and Creating the Family Spirit

In this chapter, I will be making several suggestions about how to bond in the workplace. However, let me point out that the aim of this chapter is not to make best friends out of every individual in the organization. That is not possible anyway. The aim of this chapter is to show how to create synergy in an organization when the individuals in the organization see themselves as integral parts of a whole.

Having said that, it is not uncommon to also find good friends in the workplace, so it is a good thing to always keep an open mind and heart.

Adapting to the Needs of Different Personalities

There are no two people on earth that are exactly the same. Bringing people with different personality traits together as one in the workplace is truly a challenging and complex task. That is why it calls for a careful study of the persons you lead to understand how to adapt to their needs.

Let us consider some tips on how to adapt to the needs of the different personalities in your organization.

Recognition

You will be amazed that some people who appear to be difficult are simply craving recognition and respect. They simply want to be heard or have a sense of belonging in the team or organization. A leader should take note of each member's contribution to the team and acknowledge them. It is important to teach members how to respect each other's expertise because it is different specialties that make up a team. A leader should also acknowledge the fact that every team member is a specialist in their own right.

It's Not About You

People do have internal battles which you may know nothing about. We all do. But some do not know how to mask these battles, so it shows up in the workplace and makes them appear difficult or noncompliant. This may not be true in all cases, but it is more than likely so. Armed with this understanding, a leader will make room to accommodate some behavior that tends towards being difficult. The point is to find a way to coexist with such persons in an empathetic way.

Envisage

Dominant personality traits are predictable. This is good news to a leader because it means you can truly envisage what the person will do or say and be well-prepared ahead of time to handle them. When you envisage, do it with the intention of preparing for an amicable solution or a mature way of handling the situation.

One Team; Different Perspective

A leader must bear in mind that there are as many perspectives or opinions as there are people on his or her team. There should be no attempt to muzzle people's opinions. It just shows that they care about work enough to have an opinion of how they think it something should be done. This understanding will help you to know that your team members mean well even if their opinions contradict yours.

Be Flexible

If there is one quality that can make a leader adapt

easily to different personalities in the workplace, it is flexibility. To be flexible does not mean to have double standards; neither does it mean not to be consistent. It simply means that you study how best your team members like to perform their jobs and you blend with their styles (where possible). Ask to know if they prefer texts to calls, and so on.

Adapting to the different personalities in the workplace will ensure that differences are leveraged upon to create a formidable team.

Developing a Number of Individual Relationships

Humans crave social interactions whether at work or at home. And since most adults spend more time at work than at home, it makes perfect sense to have relationships – good relationships – at work. A worker who has a good friend at work has more chances of being well involved in his or her work. They look forward to going to work because aside from job satisfaction, there is someone who they can share some degree of openness with.

Good relationships in the workplace create a conducive environment for birthing brilliant ideas.

The energy that would have been put into surmounting problems of strained workplace relationships is geared instead into productive cooperative thinking.

A leader should take time to create personal bonds with individuals on his or her team. This may seem like a far-fetched idea, but it really is not. Of course, I am not suggesting making friends with every person in your organization (unless of course, your entire organization consists of a handful of individuals). If you manage a large organization or department, there are important stakeholders in those units or teams. These are the people you directly deal or interact with and those are the people to create some level of bonding with.

Here is how to know if your relationship with your team has a good bond.

Respect

The kind of respect I refer to here is mutual respect. Your team values your ideas and you, in turn, value their opinions and inputs. This brings about implementing collective ideas to create solutions that are valuable to your organization.

Open to Differing Perspectives

One vital aspect of creating relationships with strong bonds is the ability to remain open to views, opinions, and perspectives that run contrary to your own ideas. When you learn to look at other people's opinion with an open mind to figure out if there is anything beneficial in their opinion, you demonstrate your ability to welcome contrary views.

Honest Communication

Having an open and honest communication (in writing, through emails, or verbally) is the hallmark of a good relationship. For workplace relationships to be strong there must be effective and honest communication between all the parties involved.

Thoughtful Behavior

To be thoughtful means to be mindful of the behavior that shows up as your words and actions. It is paying attention to what you say and how you act so that you do not become insensitive to those around you.

Mutual Trust

Whether in the workplace or at home, mutual trust is the basis of any good relationship. It is trust that creates the avenue for honest communication, and mutual respect. Where there is mutual trust, there will be no need to be extra vigilant about your colleagues or team members.

Getting Everyone (all those individuals) to Come Together as a Family

Creating individual relationships is good. Getting the individuals together in one strong bond is even better. This may be the solution to the chase of finding the right motivation to stimulate high performance in the workplace. If there is a strong bond in your team, the issue of mistrust is drastically minimized, and people tend to see each other as a family thereby naturally increasing performance.

There are statistics to suggest that family-owned businesses perform a lot better than other firms. This is because of the culture of value and trust that these family-own businesses inspire in their employees.

Leaders who intend to have an organization with

everyone having a strong affinity for its goals should consider the family approach in the workplace. It ensures unity and a higher level of commitment and dedication.

Here are some suggestions to help you bring individual relationships together as a family.

Involve Them

Every member of a family has a sense of belonging because they are naturally involved in family decisions and take active parts in family activities. This approach must be applied in the workplace if you desire to create a family spirit in your team. A family member who is left out from important family decisions will feel like an outcast. The employee who is not involved in any level of decision-making will also feel like an outcast.

Involve your employees at various levels of decision-making. They may not be part of the team that makes companywide decisions, but in their little way, let them feel they are part of the team also. As a matter of fact, they may not be involved in any form of decision-making at all but the mere act of keeping them duly informed gives them a sense of belonging. This is what the family spirit means.

Keep in mind that you must clearly define each team member's boundary. The family will be in serious chaos if everyone has the same responsibility as the head of the family. Boundaries help to define what is expected of each team member.

Look Out for Each Other

Families have each other's backs. That is the culture you want to establish in your team. If everyone looks out for each other, it helps strengthen the bond of unity and encourages talents to be improved upon. Employees or team members will no longer see the workplace as a place to grind but as a place that inspires personal and career development. Looking out for each other promotes trust in the workplace.

Let Them Have a Voice

The reason you have people in your team is to help you achieve what you alone cannot achieve. That means both physically and thought-wise, the power in the team is greater than yours as an individual. What then is the point of muting them? Allow them to have a voice and use it. You are paying them good money to think, so let them speak their thoughts and opinions. It may not be what you want to hear, yet it may just be the value you need.

Also, when employees feel they have the freedom to express their opinions, you will be amazed at the depth of thoughtfulness and ingenuity they will come up with. Creating a family of workers with a voice broadens your horizon and gives you several good options for handling any number of challenges.

Lay Out the Roadmap

Every member needs to see a clear roadmap for career advancement. It is a strong motivating factor to know that the company has definite plans for your advancement. When there is a transparent map for everyone to see the progressive stages in their career, there won't be cause for envy or jealousy or even a need for laying traps for colleagues.

Be Genuine, Honest and Human, and Most Importantly be Yourself

It would seem like all the qualities of being a leader are just too overwhelming! How can one person possibly possess all these qualities in order to effectively manage people? The truth is, we are all humans with shortcomings. However, the responsibility of a leader requires that they learn to absorb these qualities on a gradual basis. Always remember that leaders learn by leading.

In your honest attempt to learn the skills of leadership, be true to yourself, be authentic, and be genuine. It is true that they are people, mentors, coaches, and other leaders whose good qualities or attributes you will like to emulate, but do not lose yourself in the process. You are human, and you are meant to be uniquely you. What matters most is that you are honest and true in your learning process.

Do not fake any attribute you do not yet possess because it will be difficult to keep up the act in the face of challenges. Do not be afraid to show that you are human, and humans falter and slip several times before mastering anything. Do not feel that any sign of weakness on your part means you are a failure. Human weakness does not undermine your authority as a leader. On the contrary, the people you lead understand that you are human just like them, and any pretense to appear impeccable simply puts them off.

Admit your mistakes honestly and use them as stepping stones to learn how not to do a thing.

As a matter of fact, the more open and forthcoming you are with your shortcomings, the more accommodating others will be towards you. We are all in a constant state of learning to improve ourselves and our services to the people we lead and to humanity at large.

Allow Time for "Chewing the Fat" to Building Relationships for Effective Management

"Chewing the fat" is an essential part of human social interaction. Although it can be viewed in a negative or positive light, it cannot be entirely divorced from the workplace. Leaders are expected to be able to use these small chit-chats to properly determine each team member's dominant personality trait as well as connect more with team members on a deeper level.

Small talk is a good way to create stronger workplace relationships. Something as simple as "How's your little baby doing?" could open up a bank of personal information about your team member. This can solidify the bond between you – the leader, and the team member which ultimately is good for the organization at large.

Jumping straight into business or dishing out instructions to an employee tends to make them feel their personal wellbeing is not of any importance to the manager. It is a good practice to occasionally engage in small talk to show the team members you care.

Do not use small talk in an insincere manner, neither should you use it to merely start up a conversation. Sincerely mean it when you ask about a team member's personal welfare. Your genuineness should show up in the tone of your voice and in the expression on your face. This may sound like using company time for personal therapy sessions, but it is not. In an actual sense, it is creating a strong family bond between boss and subordinate.

Equally, do not use small talk to gather personal information about your employees to use it against them. I do not encourage gossips and that is not what I mean by chewing the fat. Gossip has a nasty way of destroying relationships, so avoid it and discourage it. Your relationship with team members will not grow stronger by gossip. Friendly chats that lead to revealing of personal information should not be used as a means for backbiting, gossip or slander.

Remember, as a manager and leader, you do have a lot of privileged information and access to people's personal lives especially when you create an environment that encourages strong bonds between you and your team. Know that they let you in on the personal information because of the trust they have in you. It is your solemn duty to keep their personal information private.

Let Them Manage Some Tasks

Giving an excellent pitch or speech about creating a family spirit and yarning about it doesn't create the family culture in the workplace. It is the actual implementation of the family culture that creates that bond.

One of the things you can begin to do to immediately show your resolve in creating a family spirit in the workplace is to allow your team to manage some tasks. Not the regular tasks in their job descriptions, but tasks that show you honestly want them to feel like part of the family. Of course, you must do this carefully and strategically so that you don't run the organization or department aground. Start with a little higher responsibility than they normally would not handle. This is a way of putting your money where your mouth is.

Summary of Key Points

The tips you have learned in this chapter include:

1. Good relationships foster collaborative efforts; it is a breeding ground for collective ideas that can lead to faster and more effective solutions.

2. Injecting a family spirit into the workplace creates strong bonds between team members and helps to motivate members as it gives them a sense of belonging.

3. Let your relationships grow beyond mere boss – colleague relationship. Allow room for your team to trust you with their personal issues as much as is comfortable for both parties.

4. Be genuine. Be real. You do not know it all that is why you are learning. A leader is humble enough to

admit his or her faults and learn from mistakes. That is honesty and genuineness.

Chapter 4:
Learn to Listen

Listen to Your Employees Concerns

You want to be a team player, so you focus your energy on building your power team. You motivate and encourage them to be focused on their tasks. You spend most part of your working hours diligently solving problems and doing your best to be a shining example of a good manager. While all these are awesome and show dedication to your duty as a manager, there is still a very vital ingredient which will drastically impact positively on your work as a manager if you apply it. It will cut down a lot of the efforts you put into motivating, solving problems, etc. This ingredient is learning to listen to those you manage – your employees, team members, or subordinates.

Listening is an art that any good manager must learn and perfect to successfully manage people in the workplace. And when I say listening, I don't mean merely hearing the words that people say. You can hear the words that people say, but the words will mean absolutely nothing to you if you are not listening. To listen means to pay attention to both spoken words and unspoken words. As a matter of fact, I did come to realize early in my job as a manager, that most of the concerns and issues that bother the staff was communicated without words. And as a manager, if you do not learn the art of paying attention to unspoken words, all the other efforts you put into your work may get you far fewer results than you had expected.

To learn to listen to those you manage, you need to apply these practical steps.

Heed All Advice

I once knew of a supervisor who always said, "I hear you." And anytime he said those words, you can be sure that is the most he would do about what was said – just hearing. I have a simple rule about listening to pieces of advice: I do not create time to hear you speak your concern if I will not do anything about what you have to say. I know that may sound too strong for some people to hear, but what is the point in clearing my schedule if all I will do is just hear you squawk? Again, how does it benefit both you and me if after hearing you out, I simply acknowledge your words and do nothing? That, to me, is a huge waste of precious time – time that both of us could have put to more judicious use.

Am I implying that a good manager of people must do something about every advice he or she gets from the people they manage? Absolutely yes! And I know that may also sound counterintuitive to some but hear me out. For every time you set aside to listen to the advice of the people you manage, ensure that you either use what they told you (if it is a good idea), or you put measures in place to be doubly sure the things they told you do not take root in your unit, department or organization. That is how to heed all advice! If the advice is what you consider as good, even if it comes in the form of criticism, it is your duty as a manager to course correct and set your organization back on the path of its stated objective. However, if the advice is what you deem bad, it behooves you to quickly checkmate such ideas. At least, someone has brought you up-to-speed with one or more ways of not achieving your goals, so do all you can to not trail that path.

If you apply this to both cases (whether good or bad advice), you have listened and have taken informed action based on what you have heard. You will not be like that supervisor whose common phrase was "I hear you."

Here is also something closely related to the above tip: do not listen for formality sake. You should not wear "that's a manager with a listening ear" as a mere tag. Do not curry anyone's favor with insincere acts of listening. Listening to the people you manage is an art, not an act! A manager should not pretend to listen. Learn to listen.

Don't Just Hear What Is Said, Listen

It is apparent to everyone that the major function of the ear is to hear words. What is not apparent is that the ear is not the only mechanism for listening to people. A manager does not just listen by hearing words alone, they listen by also reading the people they manage. So, make eye contact when the people you manage tell you about their concerns. Read their body languages – are they fidgeting? Are they uneasy? What's the look on their face? What can you tell from their moods? Are they folding their hands as they speak? Are they sitting at the edge of their seat? Do they stop speaking when someone else walks into the room? Are they speaking in a low tone? Each of these body languages is screaming the true meaning of what their words are saying. And it is your work as a manager to quickly identify what these body languages mean to effectively respond (not react) to the people you manage.

Since humans are unique, it is difficult to have a "one size fits all" meaning to their body language. However, I have used the following natural tendencies in human behaviors to help me draw a general meaning to some common body languages in the context of communication between team member and manager in a workplace.

Body Languages and Possible Meanings

Lowering of the head – this could signify hiding something or not telling the whole truth. It is also the tell-tale sign of a person who is shy, or ashamed of something.

Locked ankles – when a worker locks their ankle while talking with me, it tells me they are nervous, or they are being apprehensive. It may be that they do not want someone else (or a specific person) to walk in while they were having this conversation with me. And perhaps it could be they were nervous about the outcome of the conversation.

Folding of arms across the chest – oftentimes I get to listen to the loud screams of a worker defending their position with this body language. Of course, I don't mean screaming with the voice. This happens involuntarily most of the times but the "tells" are so glaring it gives them away. It is a way to show their disagreements.

Smiling – while this body language has generally been associated with being friendly, there is a way to detect a fake from a real smile. I once listened to someone tell me some of her concerns about her work situation. Every now and then, she pasted a smile on her face, but I wasn't fooled by it. I knew she was only trying to be polite. The sides of her eyes had no crinkles! I knew it was a fake smile.

Palms up – I have found on very many occasions, that when any of my team members talk with me with their palms facing up, they are usually communicating their honest view. I like honesty; it is a very good character trait. However, it is important for a good manager to distinguish between an honest view and a beneficial view.

Neck scratching – during meetings with your power team, make it your unwritten responsibility to keenly observe the behavior of each member of the team. You will notice that a person who begins to scratch their necks or the side of their face is likely disagreeing with something that is being said. Even if they choose not to voice their disagreement, make a mental note to talk with them after the meeting to get their genuine opinions. They may keep silent during the meeting so as not to be the odd one out.

Remember, it is not a hard and fast rule that every individual on God's green earth who displays these behaviors have the corresponding meaning attached to the behavior. As a matter of fact, there have been people who have behaved in ways that even machines that detect human behaviors find it difficult to accurately tell the true meaning of their behaviors. As one who manages people, you should take out time to study your own group of people. The best conclusions you can come up with are those drawn by yourself.

Be Stern but Considerate

It seems I am contradicting myself when I suggest that you should be stern and, at the same time, considerate. However, since we are discussing unconventional methods, it is only natural to expect seeming contradictions in this book.

It is true that managers manage men, money, and material resources (the 3 Ms) but we are majorly concerning ourselves with managing men (and women too!) in this book. The people you manage are first humans before any other title or positions they fill. They have families, they have social lives, they have feelings, and they do have challenges and problems as all humans do. With this at the back of your mind, you do not need a long sermon before you understand the need to be considerate – in fact, compassionate about the people you manage.

"That's your personal problem. Deal with it!" Have you ever been told those words by anyone who was supposed to be your leader? If you have, then you would understand perfectly how those words sting especially when you are in a not too favorable situation. You do not need to observe too hard before you notice a gradual decline in your productivity after hearing those hurtful words. And if those words were unbearable for you, how do you think any other person would feel about them? Managing people require that you put yourself in their shoes before you express your disapproval.

Practice extending the relationship with your team or employees beyond the work environment. That is one major tip that can produce amazing results. I do understand that you may not be able to have a personal relationship with every single person in your organization especially when you have a considerable workforce size. I am also not suggesting that you become good friends with everyone in your workplace. But that is where your team comes to play. As a manager, you do have an immediate team who closely works with you. Focus on creating that relationship with your close team.

When the team you head believes that you genuinely care for them, it spurs them to put in their best at work and, in that process, they exceed whatever goals set for them in their job descriptions. When your attitude communicates to them compassion, care, and consideration, your team will naturally want to reciprocate. But if they perceive (even in the slightest form) that you see them as mere tools that can be used to achieve your personal agenda of success, you undeniably no longer have a team. You merely have robots in human form working simply for the pay and not for the satisfaction of being part of the success story of your unit, department or organization at large.

Having said all that, it is still important to understand that you have an obligation to your organization. Even if you run a charitable organization, there are rules and regulations that people working there must do and abide by. Do not jeopardize your organization's goals in the guise of being considerate. There should be limits – boundaries that you cannot cross, else you become a wishy-washy manager! At all times, be sure to communicate your limits and boundaries to your team. When they clearly understand what is expected of them, they will not be tempted to take your caring demeanor for seeming weakness.

Get Involved

To really show that you are paying attention to both verbal and nonverbal communication, you should get involved with what is important to your team members. In my early days as an accidental manager, I started by giving a listening ear to my team and asking questions about the opinions they shared. But what to do next or how to proceed from that point forward was something I could not figure out. However, I quickly learned that it does no good to simply give a listening ear or ask questions and stop there. I learned that to show I truly paid attention, I must get involved by making sure they follow through with what they have explained in their answers to my questions.

You see, a manager helps to give clarity and sound perspectives to his people. When your employee or team members suggests something or raise an opinion, you should ask questions that will help shed light on such suggestions or opinions. It isn't that you didn't necessarily understand the suggestion, but you intend to help other team members gain an unambiguous understanding of the points made. The next thing is to make sure each person in the team to whom the suggestion may concern play their part to bring the suggestion to fruition. That is how to get involved. Apply this strategy and watch your team soar high.

Acknowledge

Earlier I said body language communicates a lot. What I didn't mention was that it goes both ways! As you study your people, trying to decode what they are not saying but meaning, they are equally reading you too. They read your body language and please know this: what you say means a lot to them, and what you don't say but communicate nonverbally is weightier than the words you say! Once you understand and apply this very important tip, you have yourself a major win.

But what does acknowledgment of your team have to do with listening or communicating? Here is the link. Saying "great work" when an employee or a team member accomplishes some amazing task is nice, however, a firm handshake with an eyeball-to-eyeball contact will communicate a greater degree of acknowledgment.

If you truly want to convey sincere acknowledgment as a manager, learn to also do so using body language. Learn to give an affirmative nod, to pat a shoulder, to give a quick wink, to give a warm handshake, to offer a friendly smile, and to give both thumbs up! These are gestures from a leader that means much more than words can convey to an employee. Don't let your words say "great work," while your body language screams "I don't really care who got the job done!" When you effectively convey positive gestures that are beyond words, your people know that you are listening and paying attention to them.

More than One Way of Telling You

"My door is always open," but some of your people may not be willing to walk through that open door and talk to you face-to-face. Some of your team members or employees just aren't built for such direct means of communication. If you truly want to give room for all and create a level playing field for all, you must devise other means through which the people you lead can effectively communicate with you in a way that is most suitable to their individual personalities. Be open to creative ideas even if they were sent via emails, text messages and other means of communications. A manager is good at face-to-face communication, but not all your people are managers, now are they?

One other important thing I must add here is this: don't snitch! People on your team trust you to keep their personal issues personal. They expect that if they express unfavorable opinions about other persons on your team, you are strong enough to keep sealed lips about it. One of the fastest ways I know to bring a team to its knees is for the leader of the team to tell on members. If you must succeed as a manager of people, you must avoid this dangerous trait at all costs.

Summary of Key Points

The tips you have learned in this chapter include:

1. Learning to listen to the spoken and unspoken words of the people you manage. Body language speaks volumes and communicates far more than mere words do.

2. Take informed action on both good and bad suggestions. Nurture the good ideas till they reach fruition. Ensure you put measures in place to stall or prevent the bad ideas.

3. Be involved with the activities of your team, making sure you follow through from inception to completion. Show them you care without taking your eyes off your duty. Remember, they are people too not tools.

4. Be open to team member's unique way of

communication – they have things to say, but perhaps not in your own style of communicating. Let the people you lead see that your nonverbal communication show that you are paying attention and listening to them.

Chapter 5:

Managing the Good, Bad and Ugly

People are different. Your ability to manage seemingly different people effectively is what makes you stand out as a good leader. Employees have different productivity levels in the workplace, this makes the job of managing them a bit more complex because you cannot use one method to manage all people. However, with a little bit of careful study, a manager can handle just about any employee.

In this chapter, we shall look at some tips that are sure to help you manage the different types of people in your organization or team.

Managing Good Productive Workers

If you already have productive workers, what do you do to increase or at the very least maintain their level of productivity? In what way could you manage them to ensure their productivity doesn't plummet?

Employee engagement is the key. When employees are engaged or feel they are involved in the overall success of the company, they tend to put in their best. On the other hand, disengaged employees feel disenfranchised and alienated. This invariably cost the company more to keep them on board as they tend to be liabilities instead of assets.

The truth is it doesn't necessarily require spending lots of money on perks to promote employee engagement and to keep productivity high. We shall discuss a few ways that you can use to keep the morale as well as productivity of the workers high.

Training

It is one thing to hire people to do a job, it is yet another to help them improve on ways to do the job. Training improves employee skills and, by extension, productivity. Both existing and new employees do benefit from training. Training that is tailor-made to suit employees' skill set send a clear message that says you are interested in their career development as well as their overall output. It may seem like training is geared towards using an organization's fund to develop the individual, however, if increased productivity is of any importance to the organization, training will bear desirable fruits for the organization.

Avoid Micromanaging

I do not like people hovering over me in the name of supervision. And I suppose not too many like that either. Managers who micromanage employees are saying they do not trust the employees to carry out their tasks efficiently without strict monitoring. But the fact remains that the more you micromanage people, the more they tend to falter and make mistakes because nervousness results in poor performance. To increase employees' productivity, give them directions and hands off.

Communicate Future Plans

As much as you possibly can, always keep the channels of communication open. Let there be no guessing what the plans are; the clearer you are on what is expected of your team, the better equipped they will be to help you achieve just that.

It serves little interest to dwell on the mistakes of the past, as that may be viewed as an indictment on employees' poor performance. To increase productivity, set your teams' sight on the future with clearly stated goals and how to achieve them. If you must look at past performances, let it be with the aim of highlighting the positives instead of rehearsing the negatives.

Managing Ladder Climbers

The corporate ladder is steep for some while for others it is a seemingly fast climb leaving the others wondering how they do it. Ladder climbers are those who are ambitious enough to do whatever it takes to get to the top. As a manager, be prepared to deal with such employees. They are not bad; as a matter of fact, they are the overachievers that the company needs and wants to keep. They combine a little bit of some of these personalities: the narcissist, the manipulator, and the antisocial personalities.

While these personalities are mostly seen in bad light, they possess some qualities that people can use for their advantage especially in moving up the ranks in the corporate world. For example, the narcissist personality is excellent at making a good first impression and can enthusiastically sell ideas. A manipulator personality is an expert negotiator, while the antisocial personality is good at creative thinking.

Since corporate ladder climbers tend to be overly ambitious, it is important to learn how to manage these tendencies.

Taming the Overly Ambitious

Ambitious employees are the ones who get things done in record time. They are the high performers and the crop of employees that usually make it to the top of the food chain in the workplace. They require little supervision to things done. They are good at what they do, and the organization values them as great assets.

Nevertheless, there is a tendency for them to become overly ambitious. The problem with overly ambitious employees is that they take the meaning of "initiative" too far. Often their definition of initiative crosses into the territory of usurpation. Sometimes they take a unilateral decision that they have no business taking. "Initiative" is good, but uninformed opinions leading to unilateral decisions are a bad reputation even for the most skilled employee. This overly ambitious attitude can easily pass as arrogance – indeed, it is.

It is your duty as a manager to find a balance between

their seeming arrogance and good intentions. Yes, they sometimes do have good intentions which they only know how to show by being overly ambitious. Since they are somewhat a great asset to your organization, it is wise to find a way to not come across as criticizing their good intentions in your honest attempt to nudge them back on track.

It is your job to make it abundantly clear to the overambitious employee that as much as you appreciate their skills and ability to think ahead of the pack, you also consider it important that they seek approval before acting in capacities higher than their ranks. Help them to set their career priorities right. It is also a good idea to have them coached on how best to utilize their skills.

Managing the 'Need to Be Told' People

Having enough time for your job as a manager is difficult as it is, add to that the need to always "be there" for an employee who seems to be all over you and you will get the full meaning of the word "overstressed". In every organization or team, there seems to be this one person who always needs extra attention. They are always waiting to be told what to do in ridiculously clear terms. They seem to check in every now and then to be sure they are on the right track.

How to Manage Them

It is important to first find out what is the cause of their needy attitude. Why are they not self-confident? Why do they need to be told what to do at every point? What are they afraid of? Sometimes it may be that they need to be reassured, and sometimes it could be that they may not be getting enough feedback or direction from you. Or perhaps they feel micromanaged, so they naturally check to be sure they are on track. Whatever the case, a careful reflection on your leadership style as well as the underlying reason for their needy behavior will reveal a lot.

Having established the cause of their overly dependent attitude, it is appropriate to talk with them honestly about the situation. Remember to come from a place of empathy while talking with them. Do not sound frustrated by their attitudes or be impatient in your speech. Let them know that they can do just fine without constantly checking to know what you think. The tone of your voice should boost their self-confidence. They should feel confident in their ability to perform at the end of your chats. You could say something along the lines of, "I do know you are capable of handling this task without strict supervision. You are talented in this aspect that is why you were chosen to do this." Whatever you say, do make sure it does not bruise their ego.

To effectively manage "need to be told" people, you must find a way to make them feel in charge of even the littlest of tasks.

After talking with them, make sure you listen to them and do all you can to be supportive and connect with them. Do your best to reassure them that they are doing just fine. This would go a long way to soothe the self-confidence issue.

Do also remember that some employees may want to take advantage of your openness, therefore, it is important to set boundaries with such employees. Let them understand that you have other equally important issues to attend to and cannot give them the time they wish to have with you.

Sometimes They Just Have to Be Cut Loose

"You are fired!" Those are probably the last words any manager would like to utter. We all hate to lose someone especially when they are dear to us. But in business, it is sometimes in the overall best interest of everyone involved to cut some people loose.

When a person's behavior in your organization makes you start to contemplate letting them go, it is probably best if you do let them go – there are just no two ways about it. Of course, it goes without saying that you must have given adequate room for improvement. State unequivocally what needs to be changed. Ensure that you are forthright and open about what is expected and why it is important that those expectations be quickly met. But if after lots of feedback to the employee, there is no sign of improvement or willingness to change, keeping them on your team is asking for trouble.

I learned a very valuable lesson early in my career as a manager. That lesson has helped me with a high rate of employee retention. To put the lesson in simple words: hire slowly, fire quickly. It takes a lot of work for me to hire an employee or to co-opt a member into my team. There must be a series of background checks and interviews before bringing anyone on board. However, if someone is found to have a penchant for disruption, I do not hesitate to fire them. Keeping a disruptive personality on your team is digging your own grave. Stalling or waffling is a sign of fear. For the greater good, just cut them loose and get over it!

A disruptive person is a poison to your organization. The more time you waste keeping them, the more their venom spread across your organization. In fact, others will begin to wonder why you keep such persons, thereby undermining your integrity.

Perhaps a little description will be appropriate to explain what I mean by a disruptive personality.

A disruptive personality is someone whose contribution to the overall growth of an organization is far less than the effort it takes to manage them. In other words, it requires much more energy to handle them than they're worth.

Also, a disruptive personality is someone whose attitude to work detracts from achieving the organization's goals. Instead of contributing to growth, they cause drawbacks.

Another characteristic of a disruptive personality is someone who spreads negativity among employees by causing drama or inciting negativity with their barbs. These are people who suck energy from co-workers.

If you have such persons on your team, do not hesitate to cut them loose. They do more harm than good.

Do Not Tolerate These Kinds of People

It takes different kinds of personalities to make up a good team. However, some bad eggs are better off gone from the team as quickly as possible. If not, you are looking at a potential catastrophe.

From my experience, the following kinds of persons should be cut loose without second-guessing the decision.

Those Who Disregard Conduct

Every organization has its own rules of conduct. These rules are meant to be upheld by all who work in the organization without exception. There must be consistency in enforcing the organization's rules for every member no matter their position in the hierarchy. When anyone violates the rules of conduct and the consequence requires that they are cut loose, cut them loose.

Those Who Can't Get the Job Done

The essence of hiring a person is to get them to do a job and to do it well. If after hiring an employee, they clearly fail to perform the job or somehow won't perform the job, simply fire them. There is no point keeping someone on board who is just excess luggage.

Those Who Run Down Your Business

An employee who causes more damage to the organization than they contribute or is worth has no business remaining on your payroll. The aim of business is to make a profit therefore, you cannot afford to keep someone on your payroll that continuously runs you down.

Those Who Stir Up Trouble

Some people are toxic. They just can't seem to stay out of trouble. No matter the number of times they are cautioned or warned, they somehow find a good excuse to stir up trouble among employees. Their problem is not with the job; it is with their personality.

They are often linked to almost every drama in the workplace. These are people that often-spread rumors, incite colleagues against each other, and slander the management. Get rid of such people at once.

Those Who Don't Value Clients

You will have no business without clients. One of the goals of your workers is to make and keep customers or clients. If you have anyone on board who has a bad attitude towards your clients, show them the door.

Those Who Have an Entitlement Mentality

Some people are just annoying in the way they flaunt their rights to everything. These kinds of people do not focus on their job but focus on the slightest misstep from colleagues or management so that they can table their barrages of complaints and probably claim damages or sue the company. When you notice a person with such propensity, fire them immediately. Keeping them means you are ready to spend unnecessarily on litigations and compensations for violating their so-called rights.

Summary of Key Points

The tips you have learned in this chapter include:

1. There is no "one size fits all" in dealing with employees. There are different personalities in the workplace, so tact is required in managing people of different personalities.

2. Employees who always need to be told what to do may be lacking self-confidence or feel you micromanage them. Talk to them with empathy and help them build their confidence as well as assign them more tasks.

3. Hiring and firing is part of managerial duties. You must be prepared to part ways with people who do not meet up with your organization's standard or who cause damages to your team.

Chapter 6:

How to Effectively Communicate with Everyone

In relationships as well as in business, communication is vital. However, it is not just communication in the sense of passing information but communication in a way that produces expected results. For your team or organization to thrive, you must learn and perfect the skills of effective communication. It is important for leaders who wish to be successful to know exactly when to listen and when to speak. We shall give some space to the learning of this skill in this chapter.

Communicating with Individuals and Teams

The way a skillful communicator expresses themselves depends to a large extent on the size of the audience. Talking to an individual requires a skill that is completely different from what is required to effectively communicate with an entire team. Knowing the appropriate time to deploy each skill set matters a lot.

Organization

When addressing an entire organization, it is a wise practice to always speak in broad terms or approach issues from an overall point of view. Delving into the nitty-gritty of issues should be reserved for smaller units of the organization.

Also keep in mind that you are addressing people from different specialties, and as such you should avoid jargons that are specific to a particular department. You will come across as being insensitive to others present if you begin to use specialist language peculiar to only one section of your organization. The rest will tire out easily and shut down to whatever it is you have to say. You have communicated but it was not effective enough as most others who couldn't keep up with the jargon will feel you have wasted their time. Keep your speech simple and direct.

Equally, do not give the impression that you are just delivering a speech. Let your address be tailored to allow room for responses and questions. In other words, give room for interactions during your companywide address. And also remember that every chance you are required to talk with your entire organization is a chance to deepen their trust and belief in your company. Seize those opportunities to further strengthen their faith in your organization.

Departments or Teams

If you do not want to be surrounded by a bunch of yes-men, impress it clearly on your teams that you value their opinions and you trust that they are capable of handling tasks without micromanaging them. This should be your attitude when communicating with departments or teams, especially when meeting with teams that are outside your field of specialty. After all, they were grouped into their various teams and departments for a reason; to perform specialized functions which only you cannot effectively perform.

Your aim of interacting with departments or teams is to elicit valuable information that can be directed toward improving the overall performance of the department. Hold on to that aim and your communication will be deemed effective.

One-On-One

There are no two employees that are the same, the similarity in the jobs or roles they perform notwithstanding. Therefore, it is wise never to use the same method to communicate with every single one of them. Study those you must interact with on a one-on-one basis to know how to effectively communicate with them. Generally, you will have to give people enough time to prepare for a one-on-one with you so that both parties will learn from the interaction. And keep in mind that one-on-ones are a good opportunity to further study the employee, so pay attention and learn to listen to them.

Communicating with Different Personalities

Communicating with the different personalities in your organization requires some level of good discernment as no single individual fits strictly in one personality type. A careful study, however, will reveal their most dominant personality traits. Here is how to tailor your communication to the various types of personalities in the workplace.

The Loyalist

These are the people who will never want to hurt anyone's feelings. Confrontation is never their style. They are team players.

To effectively communicate with such persons, you need to be friendly. They are easily thrown off with assertiveness or aggressive style of tackling issues. It is important to keep an even tone when talking with these types of persons. When introducing new concepts or making changes in the way things are done, do not expect them to catch on immediately. Allow adequate time for them to adjust to the changes.

The Result-Driven

These are result-oriented people. They are usually emotionally detached when taking decisions. Their eyes are fixed on goals. They are usually go-getters. Conquering is their thing – get it done with and move to the next doable thing.

To effectively communicate with such persons, you need to get straight to the point. They do not have time for small talk. Tell them exactly what you need, back off, and let them do their thing.

The Conformer

These are persons that love things spelled out to the last detail. They are dutiful and obey all rules. They are very efficient, competent and are focused on performing their tasks effectively.

To effectively communicate with such persons, leave no stone unturned when giving them details. The more facts and figures you give them, the better. These types of persons are good at procedures and can formulate new procedures using the details given to them. They are good at coming up with excellent opinions from facts, so be sure to ask for their opinions and allow them ample time to inundate you with their response.

The Interactive

These are sociable persons. They love chit-chats. All work and no play will demoralize these types of persons. They are fun to be with and are very expressive. They tend to easily deviate from course.

To effectively communicate with such persons, do all you can to approach the subject slowly. Jumping into exactly what you want to tell them with details puts them off. Be sure to always give these types of people clear deadlines when assigning them tasks. It helps them retain focus.

Transparency and Honesty

Every good leader must acquire the habit of transparency and honesty. In fact, this is a given. You cannot expect the people you lead to be honest under a dishonest leadership. They will say one thing while meaning another thus disrupting communication. Your dishonesty is sure to rub off on them.

Equally, you must be consistent. In other words, there should be no double standards with your actions or reactions. Let the people you lead know that your mood does not affect your standard; you do not allow feelings or sentiments cloud your judgments. People should not have to keep wondering if you are in the right mood before they table their issues.

Be sure to clearly define what it is you expect and communicate the same verbally and in writing. Ask questions and allow room for questions to foster a proper understanding of the tasks at hand. Do not leave tasks or projects open-ended; give specific deadlines, so that your team knows exactly what is expected and when it is expected.

And finally, have some sense of humor. The people you

manage are humans not machines. People are burdened with enough stress as it is; lightening their mood from time-to-time makes them feel at ease to approach you. If you make your work environment feel like strictly work and no room for humor, it robs your people of their human side. Remember, most of their waking hours are spent in the workplace, so create room every now and then for some good hearty laugh or at the very least a grin.

The SAS Process

The British Special Forces known as the SAS use a carefully thought-out process to deliver any task no matter how difficult it appears. The process is known as Plan, Brief, Execute, and Debrief. It is one of the best-known processes for tackling any task, and with a little bit of customizing, I have used it also in handling managerial tasks. Let us quickly take a look at how this four-step process can be implemented to bring about effective communication in the workplace.

Plan

As a manager, you need to have a clear-cut understanding of exactly what it is you intend to achieve. Just like the Special Forces, you need to detail out every aspect of your "mission" or intended task giving time, dates, who is to handle what aspect, areas to assign to who or what team, tasks to handle personally and tasks to delegate, etc. There is a saying among the Forces, "proper planning prevents poor performance." This agrees with the popular maxim we stated earlier in the section *How To Use This Book*, "if you fail to plan, you plan to fail."

Brief

This is the point where you communicate exactly what you have planned to every person involved in your planning. Be sure to expressly communicate in plain terms what needs to be done and ensure everyone involved understands their part in the whole. All parties involved should be adequately briefed; give no room for assumptions. Maintain an open channel of communication that allows for questions and responses.

Execute

Carry out the plan as intended without unnecessary deviation from plan. All unforeseen deviations arising during execution must be appropriately communicated back for possible immediate resolution. There is no second chance for a Fighter Pilot; it is either a flawless execution or crashing down in a ball of fire. Applying this principle to your mission, you do not give room for miscommunication.

Debrief

At the end of every mission or task, it is time to ask questions, get feedback, as well as give feedback. This is done with the aim of knowing what to improve, what to leave out, and new ways to better perform the task in the future. The fourth step takes into consideration necessary adjustments then dovetails to the first step again where the corrections, adjustments, and insights are put into a new plan.

A manager who inculcates and religiously implements the SAS four-step process will find that most managerial tasks can be effectively tackled with this process just as it can be used in effective communication.

Summary of Key Points

The tips you have learned in this chapter include:

1. People are not the same and it requires different ways to communicate effectively with them. One method will not work for everyone.

2. For communication to be effective, the size of the audience must be taken into consideration. What works for an individual may not be effective with an entire organization.

3. Plan, Brief, Execute, and Debrief can be used to handle most managerial tasks. For communication to be effective, it should follow the SAS four-step process.

4. Transparency and honesty are two qualities a leader cannot be divorced from. Be consistent; don't let mood swings affect your capability to show exemplary leadership. Always remember that you are human leading humans, a little bit of humor is good for business.

Chapter 7:
Feedback, Praise, Reward, and Shit Sandwiches

Feedback

In simple everyday language, feedback in the context of a workplace is a response in reaction to the performance of employees or team members. In order words, a manager measures the output of individual members of his or her team against certain organization's standards or expectations and lets them know whether they are on course or off course. It is a means to determine if there is need to course correct or stay on track or improve. Feedback could be in the positive or negative form as well as recommendations for improvements for the future. When performance is in keeping with the company's expectation or even exceeding expectations, a positive feedback is given. On the other hand, when performance is below expectation or not improving as fast as it should, critical feedback is given.

Praise, rewards (as well as awards), and shit sandwiches are forms of feedback, but before we discuss them, let us see ways through which feedback can be used effectively. I have found from my personal experience that feedback is an indispensable organizational tool which can produce desired effects if used properly. However, if used wrongly, it may lead to serious damages. I encourage you to follow the tips below to maximize the benefit of this organizational tool.

Use it on a Timely Basis

Feedback is of no use if it is not given on time. An employee performs excellently a year ago, but it takes almost a year to acknowledge their good job. That feedback is better not given after so long as it may have a very negative effect on the employee. Acknowledgments given in retrospect tend to be regarded as an afterthought, and no one likes to be regarded in such light. It sends a loud and clear message that such a person is a mere appendage that is not very important.

This applies also to negative feedbacks. If someone were to reprimand you for an offense committed several years ago, which you probably may have forgotten, it will most likely sound like a witch hunt to you. An employee or team member who missteps and has to wait for a year to know that he or she has done something wrong or has been doing something wrong throughout the year will simply take such feedback as routine. Simple logic will tell them that if they had been wrong, their actions would impact negatively on the organization's output, and the organization would not wait a whole year to course correct what it immediately could.

Therefore, this is why I refer to the Annual Performance Evaluation as prehistoric and very outmoded. This method of giving feedback is ineffective at best. It is purely a mundane routine and a colossal waste of time and energy. Why in God's name should you wait for a whole year before giving feedback on something that can be tackled right here and now? For reactions to employee's performance to have any meaningful effect, it must be done on a timely basis. As a matter of fact, there should be no strict schedule for feedback. Promptness is a vital key in feedback delivery. As they say, a delay could be very dangerous – it applies to feedback too.

Don't Avoid It, Deal with It

One huge mistake a leader should not be caught making is shying away from giving critical or negative feedback. Running from giving unpleasant feedback has a way of weakening your integrity as a manager. Many new managers fall into this trap. They dread giving negative feedback because they do not want to be the harbinger of bad news. The fear of having people turn against them so early in their career makes them avoid this vital part of managing people.

On the contrary, giving timely feedback even if it is a critical one serves to reinforce your integrity. It makes your team know that they can count on you for proper guidance in both their career and personal development. You should, however, make certain that you learn how to give critical feedback in a manner that does not counter its purpose (more on this on Shit Sandwiches).

Two-Way Street

"For a change, let me have your view about my performance." Now that is a difficult statement to make as a manager. It is normal for feedback to be a one-way thing; the manager tells his or her subordinates what they have done right or wrong. But the two-way feedback style is seldom implemented in the workplace. This is because it takes a leader with guts and a certain level of openness and willingness to both learn and listen to practice this form of feedback.

Typically, a standard (usually the company's standard) is used as the yardstick and everyone on the team is expected to give their candid opinion regarding the performance of the leader. If you want downright honest feedback, allow feedback to be a two-way thing. Now, it may not be feasible to get everyone on the team to do this face-to-face. As a matter of fact, some persons will never give you their honest opinions when they are face-to-face with you especially when they feel there is a huge gap in the hierarchy between you and them. I recommend you use a written feedback mechanism done anonymously. That is, everyone on the team writes their honest feedback without indicating their names.

If they are being honest, there is bound to be one or more recurring themes that crop up in most of the feedback. The recurring themes are what you should focus on improving upon. This is a method I have used to get honest feedback from my team. It is effective. I have found it priceless and I use it often, especially when I sense a general downturn in the productivity of my team. This two-way feedback does not curry favor and it helps you, the manager, to gauge your performance from the viewpoint of those you are leading.

For managers who are not at the top of the food chain (that is if you are not the owner of your company), it is important to listen to those above you – higher management. However, it is a bold and commendable practice to also take a sneak peek into the minds of those you are leading. You are not doing this with the aim of knowing who likes or dislike you. In fact, if you follow the recommendation to do this anonymously, you won't get to know who said what, and that shouldn't be your focus anyway. The goal is to seek for honest feedback from those you are leading – those who may not be able to walk up to you and tell you what they honestly think – in the hope of using the information you garner from them to be a better leader.

Praise and Reward

Saying the magic words "thank you," can be the difference between having a team of highly motivated performers and people who are just drooping around waiting for payday. People want to be acknowledged and recognized for their efforts no matter how little the recognition is. They want to have the satisfaction of knowing that someone sees them as an integral part of the whole. Keeping employees or your team motivated is one of the greatest single factors for employee retention.

It is not just the mere words that create the motivation, but the way the praise was delivered. Busy executives often dampen the high spirits of their team when they become too busy to take a moment to pause and properly acknowledge a job well done. It is not uncommon to hear managers spend most part of their day dishing out instructions and directives, but hardly spare a single moment to say, "nice job." As a matter of fact, many who do say words of acknowledgment immediately follow it with dishing out more instructions. That is the fastest way to dampen the morale of your team.

But why should a manager say, "thank you," when the employee is merely "doing their job?" Isn't the employee paid to do their job? True that. However, humans are not robots or machines. Being paid to do a job does not translate into employees putting their best into the job. The right form of motivation is what brings out their best. When you discover how to rightly motivate your team or employees, you will spur them into thinking and acting outside the box of their job description and give you outputs that will positively affect the bottom line of your organization.

For praise to have any meaningful effect it should be:

Spontaneous

You do not have to wait for some scheduled time to give praise. It should be a spur-of-the-moment-thing. A quick tap on the shoulder, an acknowledging nod, a thumbs-up, and "wow" do not have to wait for scheduled praise time. Spontaneity in praise shows genuineness and naturalness. It is not a mechanical act.

Specific

Give praise for something done well, not a blanket

statement like "nice job." Be specific with your commendation, acknowledgment or praise. What are you thanking them for? How well did they perform? For example: "Those were some awesome slides you pieced together in that presentation. I am impressed by your rapid improvement in presentations. You are doing a great job, keep it up." The employee hearing those words knows you paid attention during the presentation and your commendation wasn't just a formality.

Sincere

It must come from the heart for it to reflect in your body language. Say it as you mean it. People can read it from your body language if you really mean what you say. Giving praise is a hundred percent different from praise singing. When you become insincere you are merely singing praises; an act too unbecoming of a manager!

Let there be eye-to-eye contact as you give praise. Saying "thank you" or "great job" while your head is buried in your paper is a mere formality. Look into the face of the employee, give a warm smile, give a firm handshake if possible; these are signs of a sincere acknowledgment.

One more thing about sincerity: the fastest way to destroy your integrity as a manager is to give an insincere praise to an employee and then go behind their backs to tell someone you were merely playing them. Before long, the story will spread among workers and no one will ever take your commendations seriously. It is a damage that is nearly irreparable.

Special

By special, I mean, create special occasions to celebrate your team and employees. I know I have earlier suggested that praise should be spontaneous without needing to wait for some scheduled time to offer it. However, it is still a great idea to plan for special occasions when praise can be given openly.

This is where company awards events come in. A good leader does not just focus on milking performance out of his or her people; they also focus on injecting energy into their people by publicly recognizing those who have performed excellently in various aspects such the most supportive, inventive, productive or communicative members of your company.

Awards serve double duty; they motivate the recipients, and they nudge others into healthy competition. If team members know that their efforts will be duly recognized by management, there is a high chance that they will put in their very best.

Aside from awards and recognitions, praising a team member in the presence of their colleagues is a great boost for them. Practice the art of commending your team members in front of your bosses or senior management, enunciating their best qualities and how they contribute to the overall success of the organization. Remember to exclude your personal efforts when publicly praising your employees or team members. It shows selflessness and tells senior management that you recognize the effort of your team in the successes you have achieved.

Personal

A one-on-one form of praise can be very uplifting for team members. When a busy executive creates time out of their tight schedule to have a one-on-one chat with an employee with the sole aim of thanking or acknowledging their work, the effect is far-reaching. I seldom use this form of praise so that when I do it makes the event very out of the ordinary. I recommend other managers to do same. If you use this method of praise too often, it becomes trivialized and loses its effectiveness.

Include Monetary Bonuses

Financial reward is also a good way to give praise. Bonuses and incentives go a long way to motivate a lot of employees. However, care should be taken when involving monetary bonuses as a form of reward. For example, if you offer bonuses for a higher volume of products, it could lead to a reduction in quality so that quantity will increase.

Shit Sandwiches

Whatever may be said in praise of direct or brutal frankness and being forthrightly blunt, it really may not be the best technique for giving certain feedbacks. In fact, it may cause damages that are difficult to fix.

An employee whose performance has fallen below expectation may become demoralized by direct bluntness. They are certain to see it as an attack on them. This automatically puts them on the defense, and whatever corrections you intend to effect would have lost its impact. Many new managers who throw their newly found weight around in a bid to make everyone know they are now the boss, tend to fall into this misconstrued bluntness. And, as a matter of fact, some managers whose style is to be bossy are also guilty of this brazen lack of tact.

It is true that one or more team members may fall short of expectation in the execution of their jobs. It is equally true that they need to be called to order or corrected. However, the workplace is not the elementary school for God's sake! Open admonishments or reprimands in the presence of other team members or colleagues, or outright disciplinary measures for missteps is not only premature but a blatant misuse of power.

The shit sandwich method for giving negative feedback delivers the same message with a different corrective tone. It works pretty much like the sandwich – squashed fillings in between two slices of bread. The method involves squeezing something less appetizing in between two likable ideas. In this case, you commend, correct, and commend again. In other words, you look for some commendable traits about the employee or team member and praise them for that (no one is so bad that you can't find something good about them. Look for it, it's there). After the commendation, you give the negative feedback not leaving out suggestions and recommended ways that could lead to positive growth. Finally, you end with praise again.

This method has been acclaimed to keep employees' self-image intact while taking to corrections. It tells employees that you care enough to notice how good they are in some respects; however, they need to improve in some other aspect. This is a more effective method of delivering negative feedback than the prehistoric brazen honesty. Of course, other methods have been formulated that work more effectively too, however, they are improvements on the Shit Sandwich method. And I dare say it is a lot better to apply the Shit Sandwich method to deliver negative feedback than using the elementary school format.

Feed-forward

The problem with feedback is that you are always in a retrospective mode. You are simply reacting. It takes away your ability to be proactive. In other words, you cannot take the initiative with the feedback model. Feedback leaves a yawning gap for inventive ways to act rather than react. This gap gave birth to the idea of the feed-forward method.

Feed-forward is a method which promotes optimistic actionable ideas that could be applied in the future for positive results. Rather than looking back at what was done to determine if the actions taken were wrong or right, it looks forward to implementing recommendations for the future. This approach is essentially a more proactive way to checkmate the future occurrence of undesirable outcomes.

The feed-forward model of obtaining feedback from your team removes the fear of hurting anyone's feelings. Nothing in the feed-forward has happened yet, so there is no way you could possibly hurt anyone's ego. You do not need to sandwich any critical feedback or tread on eggshells while communicating your expectations to your team or employees. Using feed-forward, you are essentially shifting the focus of your team from the opinions of the "days of yore" to a critique-free promise of better days ahead.

Moreover, feed-forward encourages the entire team to contribute ideas that can move the team forward. With outmoded feedback models, the communication is only by a manager who tells his or her team what they did right or wrong and what is expected of them without any input from the team.

Summary of Key Points

The tips you have learned in this chapter include:

1. Feedback is an important tool when used promptly and correctly. When used wrongly, it is counterproductive.

2. Feed-forward is a better form of feedback. It encourages team involvement and it provides actionable steps for the future instead of always looking back to know what should have been done differently.

3. Learn and perfect the art of giving negative feedback. Done properly, negative feedback can produce the desired effect. It passes the message without necessarily bruising the ego of the employee or team member receiving the negative feedback.

4. Keep the motivation level of your team members high by regular praise and rewards. Praises should be given sincerely and for specific reasons. Saying "great job" is too general. Get specific with your praise. Let the employee or team member know that you are paying attention to them by commending specific efforts.

Chapter 8:
Managing Conflict

So long as there are humans on earth, there will be conflicts. It is completely natural, and it should not come as a surprise. Think of how bored to death you would be if everyone thought the same way. If we all liked the same things, did things the same way, and saw things the same way, this beautiful planet would have been one colossal waste! So, it is natural for people to have differing opinions and views about the same thing. When these differing opinions are expressed in ways that make another's opinion looks bad, it results in conflict. This does not necessarily mean either of the party is entirely incorrect. It simply means they have different ways of viewing the same thing without knowing how to marry their opposing views.

Leaders must be prepared to tackle this unavoidable situation with maturity. There should be no sign of playing favorites or taking sides. A leader must always maintain a neutral position when dealing with conflicts. As a leader, you must look at the positive side of the conflict, viz., it gives you an opportunity to broaden your perspective and explore opposing views.

For you to have mastered the art of conflict resolution, you would have perfected your skills in improving the working relationship among the people you lead. You would have also become highly skilled in fostering teamwork. Equally, you would be able to quickly identify and nip potential conflict engendering situations in the bud. This buys you a greater level of support from your team and your entire organization.

If you happen to have employees or team members who were able to resolve their conflicts themselves, you do not need to begin all over again to meddle into the issue. Rather, ask them how they were able to resolve amicably and use the information you gather to create a form of coaching for your team to forestall future occurrence.

Here are some tried and tested steps you can take to reach amicable conflict resolutions in the workplace. Do not just read them, apply them.

Don't Shy Away

Burying your head in the sand and pretending that everything is fine won't make the conflict go away. And looking the other way will only deepen the conflict making matters worse. If you shy away from conflict resolution because you do not want to hurt anyone's feelings, or because you want to be liked by all, you are most assuredly setting yourself up for an epic fall. A stitch in time, they say, saves nine.

Leaders who shy away from quickly resolving variances are creating a working environment of a superficial accord. The peace is simply a charade. Such false harmony is a time bomb waiting for the slightest provocation to go off, and the catastrophe is better imagined.

Confront the situation carefully but as quickly as possible. The longer you allow conflicts to linger the more havoc it wrecks and the greater the tension in the workplace. The right time to handle it is as quickly as you can gather information about the situation. In fact, the information gathering is also a vital part of conflict resolution. When you shy away from resolving conflict in the workplace, you broaden the gap between the conflicting parties; each drifting father apart from the other and before long the workplace become a breeding ground for sworn enemies.

Communication Is Key

If you lack great communication skills, you may find it extremely difficult to resolve conflicts amicably. Your ability to create an environment that supports free expression of how each person truly feels about their work is a great step towards conflict resolution. When all parties involved have a clear understanding of each other's viewpoint (without necessarily accepting same as correct), your work is half done. When you give room for clear communication and you are one step in the right direction to resolving even the most difficult of conflicts.

Do have it at the back of your mind though, that open communication comes with letting out emotions that may have been suppressed for a while. It is not unexpected to have heated talks supercharged with hurtful emotions. During such times, a leader is expected to be calm and simply listen. Listen and pay attention with empathy to each party. It is a wise practice if you arrange a separate meeting to listen to each party separately first before any attempt at bringing them face-to-face to resolve the conflicting issue.

The Right to Be Different

No two humans are meant to be exactly alike. However, because people working in the same workplace are expected to conform to certain rules and regulations, it is expected that most, if not all, should comply with these rules. Be that as it may, there are gray areas which workplace rules and regulations may not have foreseen. Therefore such gray areas are left untouched making them prone to cause conflicts. Cultural differences or social differences are some of the gray areas that may spark off conflicts in the workplace.

The best form of defense, they say, is attack. The best way to resolve conflict is to avoid it. Knowing and understanding how different the people you manage are and respecting their choice to be different can cut down on cases of conflict in the workplace. After all, conflicts arise due to a lack of understanding of the other person's perspective.

Genuine leaders are expected to respect their people's right to be different if it is not in variance with the organization's norms. When resolving conflicts, note that you are dealing with people who have strongly held points of view and as such you should not attempt to enforce upon them your own personal views. As much as possible, deemphasize your authority to create mutual trust.

No Right or Wrong

Creating a situation that is beneficial to all involved is what conflict resolution aims at. It is not an avenue for apportioning blame. Remember, no party is right or wrong, just different. The moment you start to judge or blame, you fuel acrimony and deepen the conflict.

What's the Need Here?

One very important skill you should develop as a manager is the ability to uncover people's needs. Once I learned this, I was no longer scared to face my team whenever two or more of them have conflicts. It was like suddenly I had found a magic wand that dispels all conflicts. Beyond creating the right environment and finding the most appropriate time to resolve conflicts, this skill can get you tremendous results.

Ask yourself as you listen to each party: what is the need here? What is the hidden need beyond the solution this person seeks? Why do they want this solution? Once you uncover that need your work is almost done. You can then begin to find common grounds for both parties and agree on them. Usually, when the peace talks have reached the level of finding common grounds, both parties are showing signs that they willing to shift grounds even if it is just a minute shift. Ride on that opportunity to work out a solution or solutions that meet the need you have earlier identified. In most cases, the solution both parties think they seek is not necessarily what they really sought. What they truly want is to satisfy the need which they assume their supposed solution resolves.

Finally, come to an agreement about the solutions you have reached. Ensure that all parties involved agree to the resolution. Do not assume anything at this point. Be clear that all have agreed. Do not take silence as golden in this case. As a matter of fact, silence at this point may signify that one or more parties do not agree to the resolutions.

Unresolved Conflicts

There are cases where you have taken all necessary actions to resolve a conflict, yet it stubbornly remains unresolved. And in many such cases, the conflict begins to have a negative impact on job performance as well as causing disorder and ill-feeling in the workplace. Such cases require alternative measures which may include decisions that could lead to punitive actions.

Summary of Key Points

The tips you have learned in this chapter include:

1. Conflicts are a natural part of the workplace; it is bound to happen every now and then. Do not shy away from confronting conflicts as soon as you gather your facts.

2. The aim of conflict resolution is not to apportion blame or for finger pointing. It is to find a middle path which all parties involved can tread upon without feeling wrongfully denied of their rights.

3. People have the right to be different. Respect that. Understanding the differences in people's opinion

plays a key role in minimizing conflicts.

4. Behind every conflict, there is a silent need that begs to be satisfied. Determine what need truly is and work out a solution that will satisfy that need.

Bonus Chapter:
The 40% Rule

In this bonus chapter, we shall briefly discuss an idea from a U.S. Navy SEAL named David Goggins. The idea is called "The 40% Rule." It is somewhat a simple concept to grasp, however, do not be fooled by its seeming simplicity. In practice, it requires a lot of guts and courage. It takes someone who is solely committed to being successful to retain sight of this rule in the face of mounting challenges and difficulties.

Sometimes, when faced with very difficult situations, we tend to forget all that we have learned. We simply react with a "fight or flight" instinct. And since the challenges appear insurmountable, the "fight" option quickly goes out the window, and the "flight" instinct is the only one we can hear loud and clear in such situations.

The aim of this chapter is to instill some form of mental toughness in you as a leader. Because like it or not, you will be faced with tough situations and difficult people. There will be times when you must make difficult decisions. There will be times you will feel like quitting or giving up. In such times, you must draw inspiration and strength from your reserve of mental toughness.

You're Not Done... Not Even Close

"Push!" says the doctor. But the woman lying on that bed with fists clenched and knuckles as white as snow says, "I can't do this. I'm done!" Her mind tells her it's all over. Her mind tells her she has no strength left to push... but somewhere deep inside of her, a picture of her unborn child stirs up something inside of her. She realizes she'll lose her baby and probably her life if she gives up at this crucial point. She reaches down to her deepest reserve and draws on strength. She finds she's not done yet... not even by half! She gives it her all, and suddenly a cry is heard! Her baby is born.

I have used the example of childbirth because that is the most natural excruciating experience a human can ever go through. Being a manager certainly can't be as painful as birthing another life, now can it? But if women do not give up doing what appears impossible in the moment it is occurring, why should you?

Placebo

If you have heard the expression "mind over matter," the 40 percent rule is a good example of it. It is common to assume that your toughness and strength is physical, but nothing can be further from the truth. Your toughness and strength are basically mental. "I can do it" is more powerful than your physical strength. When a person believes that they can do a thing, it is very difficult to get them to back down from doing that thing. When you eventually get your mind into a state of believing, you become stronger than anything physical – that is, all matter.

I have heard of the placebo effect and how science and medicine use it for the positive psychological effect it has on patients because of their beliefs. Before I started writing this and the two preceding chapters, I was physically exhausted from a long day. However, I was determined to finish writing this chapter though my body was screaming at me to go to bed. I drank some coffee in the belief that it would keep me awake to complete the writing of this chapter and the rest of this book. Interestingly, six hours past my bedtime, I was still fully awake, alert and writing! Now, I can't tell if it was the coffee working or if it was my belief that the coffee will keep me awake that kept me awake. The reason I say that is because I had taken coffee at other times and still dozed off right after drinking it. But on this occasion, it did work.

The point here is simple: if you convince yourself that you can achieve something, that mental toughness will overcome any physical weakness. This is a key point to remember because it will keep you going in your work of managing people. When you feel like giving up, ask yourself what percentage of your inner toughness you have used. The 40 percent rule suggests that at the point where you feel like giving up, you've probably just used only 40 percent of your ability. If you develop the "I can do it" mentality, it fuels you beyond the 40 percent mark. On the other hand, "I can't do it," truncates whatever drive you had left in you. Those who have pulled through no matter how difficult the situations and circumstances appeared to be, were those who believed that they too can do it.

The task of leading people requires a certain level of mental toughness, the kind which demands that you constantly dig deep and tap into your inner reservoir of strength. We all have this reservoir. It is deep within us. And it patiently awaits our willingness to call it forth and use it to our maximum benefit.

Purpose

One thing that is sure to keep you going when motivation fails is "purpose." Why are you doing what you are doing? Why did the mother get pregnant in the first place? When the motivating voices of the nurses and doctors fail to provide her strength, she still found strength when she reflected on the reason, she got pregnant. Why do you want to succeed as a manager? How is becoming a great leader significant to you? What is required to accomplish that goal? What is your purpose? If your purpose is greater than you, it will keep you going even in the face of tough challenges. Situations that can obliterate motivation will not touch your purpose, you know why? Motivation is external. Purpose comes from within – it is inspired from the inner parts of your being, therefore, nothing external can exterminate it except you permit it.

As you strive to apply the tips, steps, and suggestions in this book, ensure you frequently remind yourself of your purpose. This helps you get over whatever feeling of inertia you may have about acting on what you have learned. When procrastination knocks on your door, purpose tells it you are not in. When fear of failure stares straight in your eyes, it is your purpose that gives you the courage stare it down. And when the situation and the people in your workplace appear unmanageable, it is purpose that whispers, "You can do it."

Can You See It and Feel It? Then You Can Achieve It

Just like the pregnant mother who drew strength from the mental image of her unborn child, if you can see yourself clearly in your mind as having overcome whatever challenging situation you are faced with, you are going to triumph over that situation. In other words, no matter the difficulty you face, you must visualize yourself as a success long before any physical appearance of success shows up in your current reality. If you hold that picture of success in your mind's eye and never back down from it, success is the only possible outcome you can experience.

Visualizing is a bit different from mere imagination or wishful thinking in the sense that visualizing contains one vital ingredient which wishful thinking or mere imagination do not have. That ingredient is feeling or emotion. When I suggest that you visualize yourself as a success, it means you should add emotions to your vivid imaginations. Do not just see it; feel as though it is happening, or it has happened. I know this may sound like some psychic or extrasensory mumbo-jumbo, but the results are fascinating when you apply these simple techniques.

Although the 40 percent rule, visualization, and the likes are for the most part supported by narratives of personal experiences rather than a lot of scientific evidence, it is difficult to disprove the fact of mind over matter.

Summary of Key Points

The tips you have learned in this chapter includes:

1. When you think you are done, you've probably used only 40% of your mental toughness.

2. Your strength is more mental than it is physical. If you convince yourself that you can achieve anything, you can.

3. Purpose comes from within. It will keep you going when motivation reaches its limit.

4. See it, feel it, and you can have it. When you create a clear image of what you want to achieve in your mind, no matter how impossible it is in the present moment, and you add the emotion that comes with accomplishing that goal, you are absolutely going to achieve it.

Final Thoughts

At the beginning of this book, in the introduction to be precise, I did point out that managing people could be a tough job. However, if someone like me who had no formal training in the art of managing people could become a successful manager, I do honestly think you can manage people too.

It takes dedication and commitment to do this, but then, what is there on God's green earth that anyone could ever become good at without some level of dedication and commitment? Commitment is not peculiar to someone who wants to be a successful manager alone. Even in the most simple and basic things such as a child learning how to eat with a spoon, a certain level of commitment is required as the child struggles at first with the spoon and then with the food creating a mess just to get it right. Without dedication and commitment, that child is bound to give up. But the child sees other humans eating with a spoon and is inspired to do same. If others can, so can it too.

Here's a principle I suggest you should use as your

guide: if others can, you can too. The week and feeble-minded get jealous and feel threatened by the success of others. The dedicated and committed feel inspired by the success of others. There were times I felt intimidated by the idea of leading a group of people some of whom were older and more experienced than I am. There were times I felt overwhelmed by the enormity of the task that sat squarely on my shoulders. There were times I felt debilitated by indecisions. But through all these tough times, the thought that others have done this before and that I could do it too kept me going.

Being called to a position of authority where suddenly you are the center of attention can be daunting and scary. The tendency to misstep and falter is high. You can become immobilized by the fear of stirring the hornet's nest – the temptation to leave things the way they were in order not to hurt anyone's feeling is enormous. However, you must realize that for situations to change, for people to change, you first must change. When the change starts from you, the people you lead will follow suit and situations will morph to conform to the attitudinal changes in your workplace.

The work of managing people is essentially a personal development journey for the manager. No one can truly give what they do not have. For a manager to successfully deliver leadership to the people he or she leads, there must be an internal transformation or development that takes place and continues to take place. I have attempted to highlight some of these transformations in this book. They are written in form of tips and steps to take in order to succeed in your career as a manager. However, they are not just temporal band-aids; they are steps that will unquestionably lead to internal changes in the individual who applies them.

This book is pragmatic. Theories (of which I am not too good at) have been greatly minimized and emphases were placed on practical steps, methods, techniques, and tips. These are some of the very steps I took which helped me succeed in my career as a Construction Manager. I strongly suggest you read this book more than once. If you have read it from start all the way to this point, I congratulate you. You can now begin to study it, concentrating more on the chapters that you feel you need to learn more about.

I wish I had all the information in this book earlier in

my career as a manager. It took several years of trial and error to come to some of the conclusions contained within its pages. I urge you to apply what you have learned and watch your career as a manager soar.

With a little bit of consistent practice, you can manage people, too!